BLUE SKY
WHITE STARS

UN CIELO AZUL
BLANCAS ESTRELLAS

SARVINDER NABERHAUS

Illustrated by · Ilustrado por
KADIR NELSON

Bilingual edition adapted by   Edición bilingüe adaptada por
TERESA MLAWER

DIAL BOOKS FOR YOUNG READERS

BLUE SKY
WHITE STARS

UN CIELO AZUL
BLANCAS ESTRELLAS

Blue sky

White stars

Azul celeste

Blancas estrellas

Red rows
Hileras rojas

Red rows
Franjas rojas

WHITE ROWS
ESTELAS BLANCAS

White rows
Franjas blancas

RED, WHITE, AND BLUE
ROJO, BLANCO Y AZUL

OLD GLORY
ESPLENDOR Y GLORIA

OLD GLORY

ESPLENDOR Y GLORIA

Sea waves
Un mar de ondas

SEE WAVES

UN MAR DE ONDAS

SEW TOGETHER
WON NATION

PUNTADA A PUNTADA
UNA NACIÓN

So together, One nation
Todos unidos, Una nación

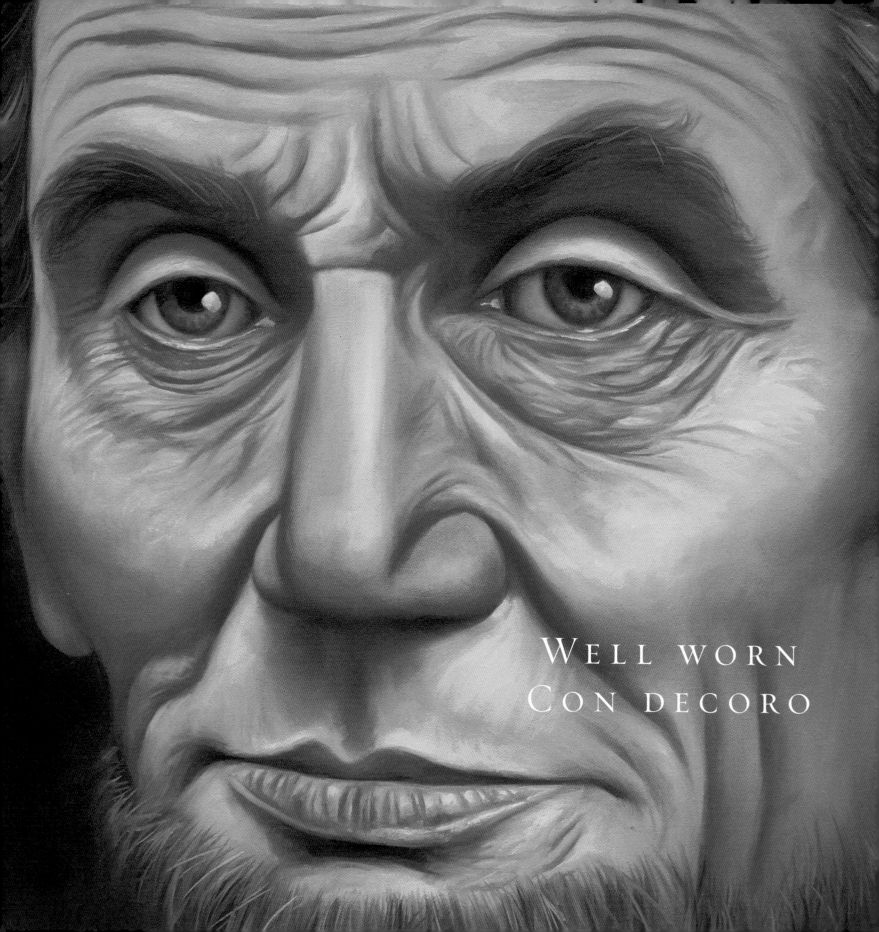

Well worn
Con decoro

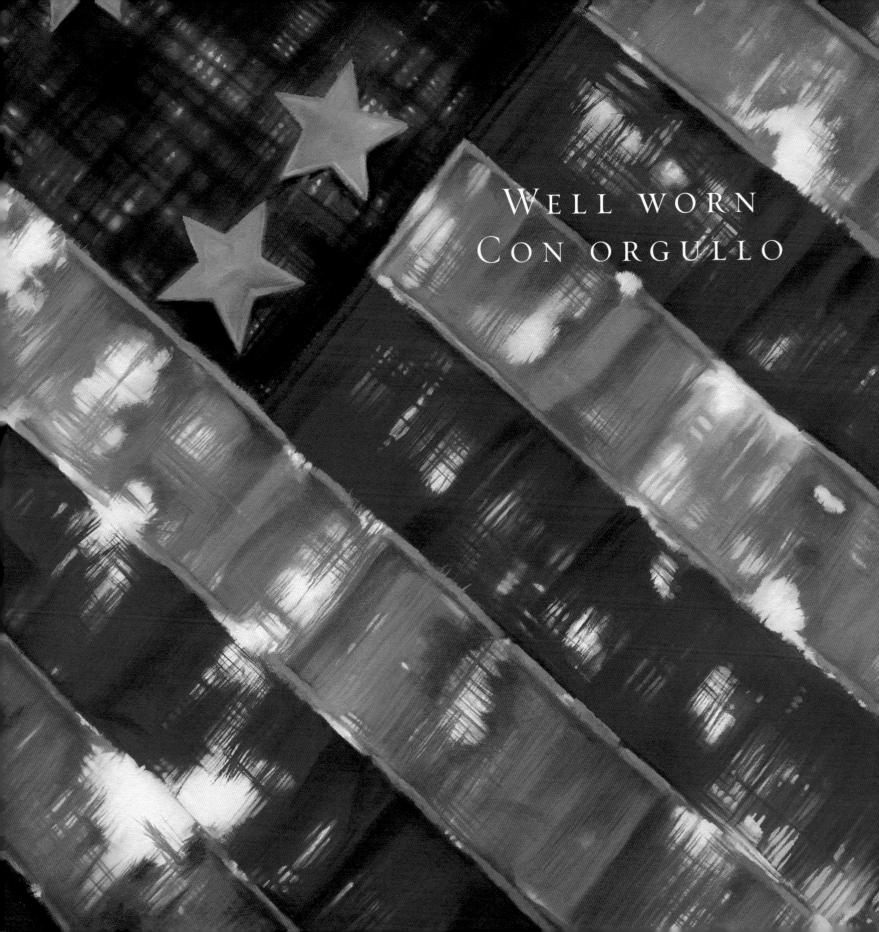

WELL WORN
CON ORGULLO

WOVEN TOGETHER
ENTRELAZADOS

WOVEN TOGETHER
ENTRELAZADOS

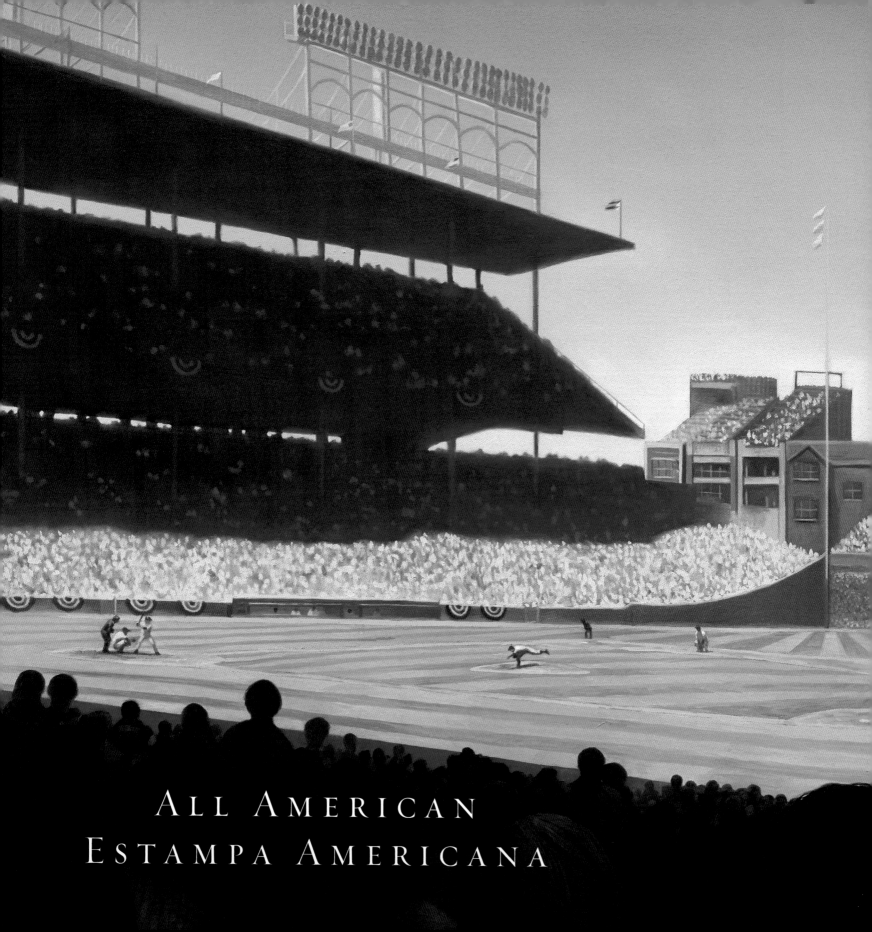

ALL AMERICAN
ESTAMPA AMERICANA

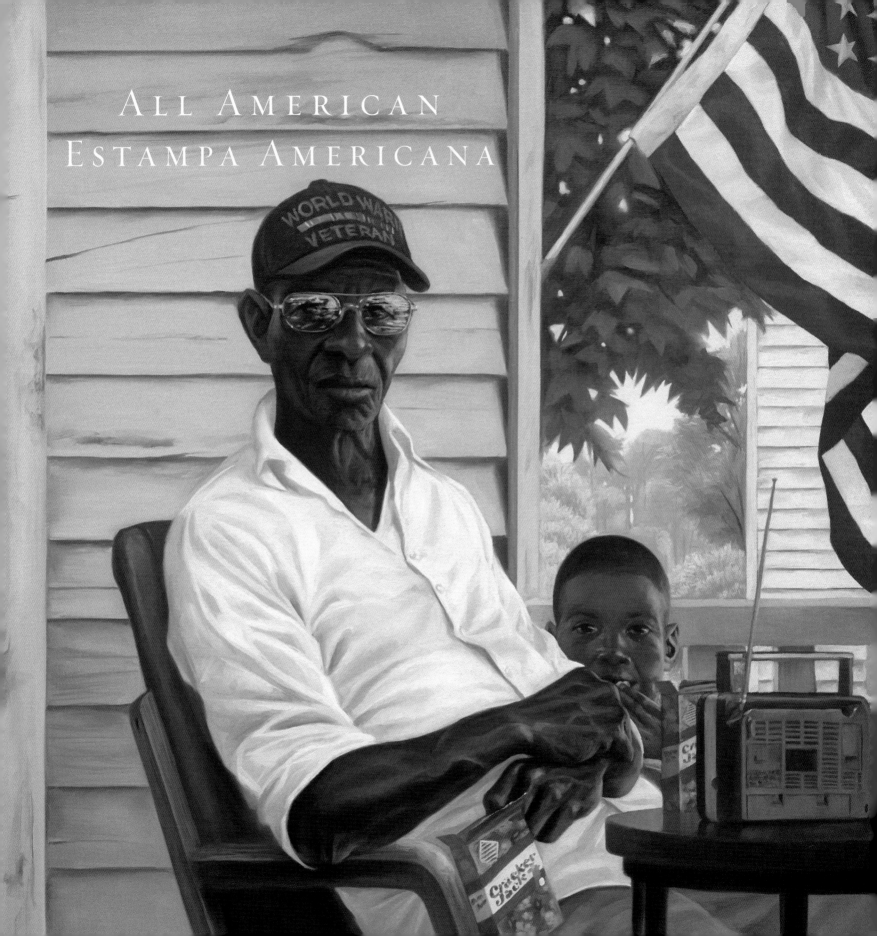

ALL AMERICAN
ESTAMPA AMERICANA

STAND PROUD
CON ORGULLO

STAND PROUD

CON ORGULLO

RISING UP
SE ELEVA

RISING UP
SE ELEVA

Fly high

Asciende alto

FLY HIGH
ASCIENDE ALTO

FREEDOM
LIBERTAD

RED, WHITE, BLUE SKY, WHITE STARS

ROJO, BLANCO, UN CIELO AZUL,
BLANCAS ESTRELLAS

FOREVER
POR SIEMPRE

To Goga, Jyoti, Nick, Tom, and Ruth, and all the generations of immigrants —S.N.

A NOTE FROM THE AUTHOR

This story was written as a parallel between America and its flag—the same words describe both. I began this book thinking of the deep blue sky dotted with white stars that early immigrants to this country saw as they boarded ships headed toward religious freedom in the New World.

In the early 1920s my great-grandfather, Boota Singh Bal, boarded a ship to come to America but at the last minute changed his mind. My dad wished he had stayed on the boat and embarked on the journey. It was my dad's dream to come to America, which he achieved through a veterinary medicine scholarship. In 1965, when I was nearly four years old, my family left Punjab, India, and traveled over 7,000 miles to join my father. Thus began my lifelong journey assimilating into the culture that fostered the American dream, eventually becoming a citizen in 1996. Like my dad, I've followed my dreams which led me to this story, where blue sky is filled with white stars.

ACKNOWLEDGMENTS

I want to acknowledge Ann Green for her immeasurable help with *Blue Sky*. I also want to acknowledge the Bal family, Harpal and Harbhajan, who brought me to this country; my kids and husband, as well as the Randhawa family and Naberhaus family. A special thanks to Lucia Monfried, Lauri Hornik, Jenny Kelly, Kadir Nelson, Ammi-Joan Paquette, my online critique groups, Write Away (Jody, Sandy, Suzanne, Jill, Kerry, Diana) and the Ames group (including Susan Schmid).

NOTES PROVIDING BACKGROUND MATERIAL ABOUT THE FLAG AND OTHER PATRIOTIC SYMBOLS AND THE MEANING OF THE PHRASES IN THIS BOOK ARE AVAILABLE ON THE AUTHOR'S WEBSITE.

A Goga, Jyoti, Nick, Tom y Ruth, y a todas las generaciones de inmigrantes —S.N.

NOTA DE LA AUTORA

Esta historia es una analogía entre la nación de Estados Unidos y su bandera—las mismas palabras, o similares, en el caso de esta edición bilingüe describen a ambas. Comencé este libro pensando en el intenso cielo azul, salpicado de blancas estrellas, que los primeros inmigrantes quizá vieron al embarcarse hacia el Nuevo Mundo en busca de libertad de religión.

A principios de la década de 1920, mi bisabuelo, Boota Singh Bal, subió a bordo de un barco con destino a América, pero en el último minuto se arrepintió. Mi padre hubiera preferido que se hubiese quedado en el barco y emprendiera el viaje. Mi padre siempre soñó con venir a América, lo cual finalmente logró gracias a una beca que recibió para estudiar Medicina Veterinaria. En 1965, cuando yo tenía casi cuatro años, mi familia dejó Punjab, India, y viajamos más de 7,000 millas para reunirnos con él. Y así comenzó mi recorrido por la vida, asimilando la cultura que fomentó mi sueño americano hasta hacerme ciudadana en 1966. Al igual que mi padre, yo perseguí mis sueños hasta llegar a esta historia, donde un cielo azul aparece cubierto de blancas estrellas.

AGRADECIMIENTOS

Deseo dar las gracias a Ann Green por su inconmensurable ayuda con *Blue Sky*. También quiero expresar mi agradecimiento a la familia Bal, Harpal y Harbhajan, por traerme a este país; a mis hijos y a mi esposo, así como a las familias Randhawa y Naberhaus. Un especial agradecimiento a Lucia Monfried, Lauri Hornik, Jenny Kelly, Kadir Nelson, Ammi-Joan Paquette, y a mis grupos de críticos en línea, Write Away (Jody, Sandy, Suzanne, Jill, Kerry, Diana) y al grupo Ames (incluyendo a Susan Schmid).

FOR EVERY AMERICAN, LIFE, LIBERTY, AND
THE PURSUIT OF HAPPINESS
—K.N.

A TODOS LOS ESTADOUNIDENSES,
A LA VIDA, LA LIBERTAD Y LA BÚSQUEDA
DE LA FELICIDAD. —K.N.

A NOTE FROM THE ILLUSTRATOR

I am very proud to have created this series of paintings illustrating Sarvinder Naberhaus's poetic celebration of the American flag. I was immediately struck by the author's sparse yet rousing text—its simplicity and power; its beautifully drawn parallels between the American landscape and the diversity of its people, and the symbolism stitched into the fabric. It is the American ideals that have continued to echo in our hearts and minds throughout our tumultuous history.

With each painting, I was inspired to remind readers of the resilience of American principles, and that as we continue to push forward, our strength lies in our willingness to embrace our differences. I hope this work will always remind us that our ever-evolving country was forged by—and for—people from all walks of life and every background, and that our future as a nation hinges on Abraham Lincoln's enduring admonition that, "a house divided cannot stand." The American flag is a shining symbol that calls us to remember that we have the potential to uphold the promise of "Life, Liberty, and the Pursuit of Happiness," together. Only together . . .

NOTA DEL ILUSTRADOR

Me siento muy orgulloso de haber creado las pinturas para ilustrar las poéticas palabras de Sarvinder Naberhaus, en honor a la bandera de Estados Unidos. Me impresionó el texto, de pocas pero conmovedoras palabras, de la autora: su simplicidad y poder; la belleza de la analogía entre el paisaje de Estados Unidos y la diversidad de su pueblo, y el simbolismo tejido en su fibra. Son esos ideales americanos los que siempre han resonado en nuestros corazones y en nuestras mentes a través de nuestra tumultuosa historia.

Con cada dibujo quise que los lectores tuvieran presente la firmeza de los principios de Estados Unidos, y que, según nos vamos abriendo camino, nuestra fortaleza radica en nuestro deseo de aceptar y respetar nuestras diferencias. Es mi esperanza que esta obra nos recuerde que nuestro país, en constante evolución, fue forjado por—y para—gente de diversos ámbitos y procedencia, y que nuestro futuro como nación depende en la sensible amonestación de Abraham Lincoln: «una casa dividida no puede sostenerse». La bandera de Estados Unidos es un símbolo radiante que nos recuerda que la promesa de «vida, libertad y la búsqueda de la felicidad» depende de todos nosotros, juntos. Y solamente juntos . . .

Dial Books for Young Readers · Penguin Young Readers Group
An imprint of Penguin Random House LLC · Visit us at penguinrandomhouse.com

Text copyright © 2017 by Sarvinder Naberhaus. Illustrations copyright © 2017 by Kadir Nelson.

Penguin supports copyright. Copyright fuels creativity, encourages diverse voices, promotes free speech, and creates a vibrant culture.

Thank you for buying an authorized edition of this book and for complying with copyright laws by not reproducing, scanning, or distributing any

part of it in any form without permission. You are supporting writers and allowing Penguin to continue to publish books for every reader.

CIP Data is available. Printed in China | ISBN 9780803737006

Special Markets ISBN: 9780525553052 Not for resale

7   9   10   8   6

Design by Jennifer Kelly | Text set in Requiem Fine

The interior artwork was created in oils on canvas. The front and back covers were created in oils on panel.